CONTENTS

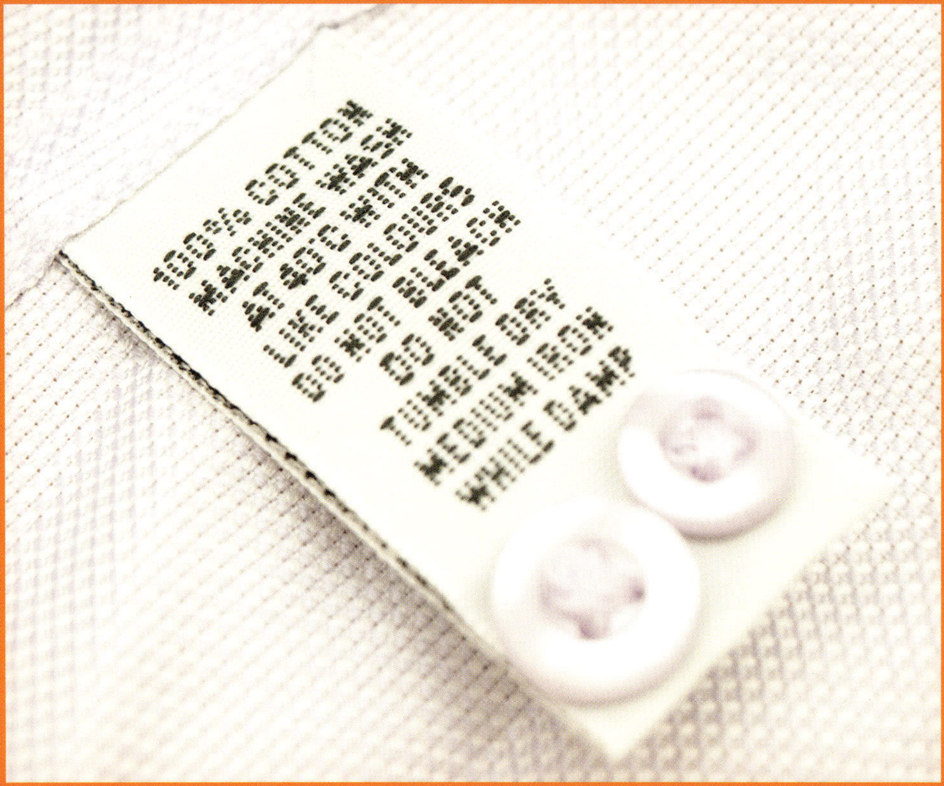

A label tells you what clothes are made of.

Look at the Label

Do you wear T-shirts? Look at the label of a T-shirt. Does it say it is made of cotton? You are wearing a plant!

Cotton is just one plant that is used to make clothes. Let's take a look at plants we wear.

Cotton bolls open up when the cotton is ready to be picked.

Cotton Plants

A cotton plant grows flowers. The flowers fall off and leave seed pods called **bolls** behind. The bolls have seeds inside.

Make a Guess!

Find five pairs of pants. Guess how many of them are made from cotton. Write down the number. Now look at the labels. Was your guess correct?

Bales of cotton are ready to be made into fabric.

White **fibers** grow from the seeds. The boll opens when the fibers get big. The fluffy fibers look like white cotton candy!

The cotton fibers are picked. A machine called a **cotton gin** cleans them. The fibers are pressed into **bales**.

Cotton yarn is made into fabric.

The bales of cotton are sent to a **textile** mill. The cotton is turned into **yarn**. The yarn is made into **fabric**. The fabric is sent to a factory that makes clothes.

Think!

What else is made out of cotton? You might use cotton every day. Do you use cotton balls or cotton swabs? Do you sleep on cotton sheets?

The flax plant is used to make linen fabric.

Other Plants We Wear

Some clothes are made from a fabric called **linen**. Linen is made from the fibers of **flax** plants. The fibers come from the tall stems of the plants.

There are some other plants that are used to make clothes, too.

Bamboo is a tall grass. It grows very quickly.

Bamboo can be made into fabric. The leaves and other soft parts of bamboo are made into yarn. The yarn is made into fabric. The fabric is made into clothing.

Look!

What types of fabric do you have in your house? Look at the labels of your sheets, tablecloths, and towels. Is anything made of cotton, linen, or bamboo?

The stems of plants are woven into straw hats.

From Head to Toe

Have you ever seen a hat made from straw? A hat can be made from the leaves of palm trees. It can also be made from the stems of plants. Dried plant stems are woven together to make many items we wear.

Latex drips from a rubber tree tap.

The rubber in your shoes may come from rubber trees. Rubber trees have a liquid inside them called **latex**.

Cuts are made in the bark of the rubber tree. The latex oozes out from the cuts. The latex is made into rubber. The rubber can be used to make shoes.

Look at the labels inside clothes when you go shopping.

Do you know what you are wearing? Look at the labels. Many clothes are made from plants. Are you wearing plants?

Ask Questions!

Ask a **librarian** to help you find facts about the clothes you wear.

GLOSSARY

bales (BAYLZ) large bundles of things such as cotton or hay

bolls (BOHLS) the parts of cotton plants that hold the seeds

cotton gin (KOT-uhn JIN) a machine that separates the seeds from the cotton fibers

fabric (FAB-rik) a cloth made by weaving fibers together

fibers (FYE-burz) long, thin, tough threads of something

flax (FLAX) a plant with long, strong fibers that can be made into linen

latex (LAY-tex) a milky liquid that comes from certain plants and is used to make rubber

librarian (lye-BRAR-ee-uhn) a person who works in a library and helps people find books and information

linen (LIN-uhn) fabric that is made from the fibers of the flax plant

textile (TEK-stile) fabric that has been woven or knitted from yarn or thread

yarn (YARN) fibers that have been twisted or spun into long strands for weaving or knitting cloth

FIND OUT MORE

BOOKS

Garcia, Tracy J. *Eli Whitney*. New York: PowerKids Press, 2013.

Nelson, Robin. *From Cotton to T-Shirt*. Minneapolis: Lerner Publications, 2013.

WEB SITES

Cotton Counts—The Story of Cotton

www.cotton.org/pubs/cottoncounts/story/
Learn about the history of cotton.

Cotton's Journey—Watch Cotton Grow

www.cottonsjourney.com/watchcotton/
Look at pictures that show cotton plants from seedling to harvest.

Plant & Us—Plants & Fashion

www.plantsandus.org.uk/fashion.htm
Find out about the top 10 plants that are used to make clothing.

INDEX

ABOUT THE AUTHOR

Jennifer Colby is a school librarian, and she also has a bachelor's degree in Landscape Architecture. By writing these books, she has combined her talents for two of her favorite things. She likes to garden and grow her own food. In June she makes strawberry jam for her children to enjoy all year long.